TECHNICAL REPORT

Measuring and Understanding Economic Interdependence in Allegheny County

Sally Sleeper

Henry Willis

Eric Landree

Beth Grill

Prepared for the Heinz Endowments

INFRASTRUCTURE, SAFETY, AND ENVIRONMENT

The research described in this report was conducted for the Heinz Endowments by RAND Infrastructure, Safety, and Environment (ISE), a unit of the RAND Corporation.

Library of Congress Cataloging-in-Publication Data

Measuring and understanding economic interdependence in Allegheny County / Sally Sleeper ... [et al.].
    p. cm.
    "TR-200."
    ISBN 0-8330-3709-9 (pbk.)
    1. Income—Pennsylvania—Allegheny County. 2. Allegheny County (Pa.)—Economic conditions.
I. Sleeper, Sally.

HC107.P43I515 2005
339.2'09748'85—dc22

2004026857

Published 2004 by the RAND Corporation
1776 Main Street, P.O. Box 2138, Santa Monica, CA 90407-2138
1200 South Hayes Street, Arlington, VA 22202-5050
201 North Craig Street, Suite 202, Pittsburgh, PA 15213-1516
RAND URL: http://www.rand.org/
To order RAND documents or to obtain additional information, contact
Distribution Services: Telephone: (310) 451-7002;
Fax: (310) 451-6915; Email: order@rand.org

Preface

In December 2003, the Program on Economic Opportunity at the Heinz Endowments asked the RAND Corporation to continue to research issues of governance by exploring the degree and nature of economic interdependence within Allegheny County. This report provides evidence on how Allegheny County's 130 municipalities are interconnected, as people commute across municipal borders to work, creating interregional economic flows. This report is useful to community and business leaders who are engaged in meaningful discussions about what it means to be a region.

This research was conducted within RAND Infrastructure, Safety, and Environment (ISE), a unit of the RAND Corporation. The mission of ISE is to improve the development, operation, use, and protection of society's essential man-made and natural assets; and to enhance the related social assets of safety and security of individuals in transit and in their workplaces and communities. The ISE research portfolio encompasses research and analysis on a broad range of policy areas including homeland security, criminal justice, public safety, occupational safety, the environment, energy, natural resources, climate, agriculture, economic development, transportation, information and telecommunications technologies, space exploration, and other aspects of science and technology policy.

Inquiries regarding RAND Infrastructure, Safety, and Environment may be directed to:

Debra Knopman, Director
1200 S. Hayes Street
Arlington, VA 22202-5050
Tel: 703.413.1100, extension 5667
Email: ise@rand.org
http://www.rand.org/ise

Contents

Figures and Table

Figures

Table

Summary

As part of its ongoing interests in economic development opportunities in southwestern Pennsylvania, the Program on Economic Opportunity at the Heinz Endowments asked RAND to explore the degree and nature of economic interdependence within Allegheny County.

This report characterizes economic interconnections through the flows of earnings of full-time workers who cross municipal boundaries in Allegheny County. Our analyses reveal a dense web of economic flows that closely tie the municipalities of Allegheny County to the City of Pittsburgh and to one another. We describe this economic interdependence among the municipalities in Allegheny County and examine how the municipalities are interconnected with the City of Pittsburgh.

The analyses of earnings are based on where people live and work. We construct simple metrics to estimate the amount of earnings from workers who live and work within their community and those workers who bring their earnings home from other jurisdictions. Our analyses show that ten municipalities have estimated *net* deficits in earnings of more than $100 million, with the City of Pittsburgh at over $5 billion. Another fifteen municipalities have *net* surpluses in earnings of more than $100 million.

The flow of earnings across municipal boundaries is used to describe the degree of economic interdependence in Allegheny County. We find that 80 percent or more of the total earnings flowing into county municipalities are generated by jobs outside a municipality for 114 municipalities (88 percent). Further, 124 of municipalities (95 percent) in the county "export" 60 percent or more of earnings from jobs within their municipality to non-resident commuters. The amount of earnings flowing across the boundaries of municipalities is not surprising given that, on average, only 13 percent of residents work within their own municipality.

The City of Pittsburgh is the most financially distinctive municipality in the county in terms of the amount of earnings exported outside its borders. The city alone accounts for more than one-third of all exported earnings of the 130 municipalities combined. We find that 63 municipalities (49 percent) "depend" on the city for 30 percent or more of the earnings of all residents in a municipality. That means, for every dollar earned by residents in one of these municipalities, 30 cents is generated by jobs within the City of Pittsburgh. Only nine municipalities receive less than 15 percent of total earnings from jobs within the city.

This report describes the economic interdependencies among Allegheny County municipalities for earnings. The information is an important input into discussions about the economic viability of the region as municipalities struggle with budget issues and compete for the same workers and jobs. Understanding how, and the extent to which, municipalities depend on one another and the city can support the discussions currently under way about city-county consolidation, issues of taxation and tax sharing, and more generally, how to make economic decisions as a region.

Acknowledgments

We would like to thank the many members of the RAND research staff who helped us in the refinement of the ideas within this report, including but not limited to participants at the RAND-Pittsburgh Research Seminar, Barry Balmat, and Debra Knopman. We also greatly appreciate the comments from our reviewers, David Shlapak of the RAND Corporation and Jerry Paytas of Carnegie Mellon University's Center for Economic Development, who provided insightful comments and critically improved the report. We appreciate the hard work of our programmers, Chris Fitzmartin in constructing the data sets and Michael Tseng for his Geographic Information System (GIS) expertise. We also are grateful for the hard work of our support staff, Lisa Sheldone, Christina Pitcher, and Stephanie Sutton. Invaluable in our research process were the contributions of knowledge and insight provided during our meetings and discussions with business and community leaders. We also would like to thank Brian Kelley and the Heinz Endowments for sponsoring our research.

Measuring and Understanding Economic Interdependence in Allegheny County

Introduction

In December 2003, the Program on Economic Opportunity at the Heinz Endowments asked the RAND Corporation to explore the degree and nature of economic interdependence within Allegheny County.

This report demonstrates that there is a dense web of economic flows that closely tie the municipalities of Allegheny County to the City of Pittsburgh and to one another. The web is created through vast numbers of workers in Allegheny County who live in one municipality and work in another, meaning that enormous sums of income are flowing back and forth across jurisdictional lines. Similar to the other municipalities, the City of Pittsburgh is integral to the web when it comes to attracting commuters. However, the city is the lone exception in not "exporting" its residents as workers to other jurisdictions, with nearly 70 percent of city workers working within its boundaries, as compared with an average of less than 15 percent of workers in the other municipalities working within their own municipalities. Moreover, Pittsburgh is the economic engine of the county, with jobs in the city accounting for over one-third of *total* commuter earnings in the county and at least 15 percent of the commuter income in 116 of 130 municipalities.

The earnings interdependencies in the county have implications for a host of issues, including how to manage economic development and growth in Allegheny County, which in turn plays into decisionmaking about business location, taxation, and improving the quality of life for residents. The prevalence of the inter-jurisdictional income flows shown in this report suggests that communities have little control over their own prosperity, with their economic fates inextricably tied to the fortune of other municipalities. A fragmented approach to economic development may invite competition for the same slices of the existing pie—whether in the form of jobs or residents—resulting in rearranging the slices but not enlarging the pie.

The question of what it means to make economic decisions as a region is particularly pressing today because of the fiscal pressures facing the city, county, and many of the municipalities. This report provides a common understanding of how municipalities in Allegheny County are economically interdependent in order to allow productive discourse about what it means to be a region, and about which issues are local and which are more fundamentally regional.

We examine economic interdependence among municipalities based on an analysis of earnings and employee flows across municipal boundaries. In this report, we analyze the economic interdependency of municipalities within Allegheny County and the nature of the dependency of the municipalities on the City of Pittsburgh.

Measuring Income Flows and Economic Interdependence in Allegheny County

RAND set out to analyze the economic flows and interdependencies by first collecting information on where people live, work, and what they earn.[1] Using Census data and graphical approaches, we describe the primary flows of median earnings of full-time workers employed year round at a municipal level throughout Allegheny County. The data sources for the analyses are further discussed in the Appendix.

Characterizing and Measuring Income Flows and Interdependence in Allegheny County

We begin by defining the three basic building blocks of the earnings analysis followed by additional metrics used in the analyses: domestic, imported, and exported earnings.

Basic Building Blocks. Consider the mythical borough of Grand Fenwick. Earned income flows to and from it in three ways. First, some residents of Grand Fenwick work within the borough itself. We refer to their earned incomes as Grand Fenwick's *domestic earnings*. The rest of Grand Fenwick's employed population work outside of the borough, in other municipalities, and bring their paychecks home to Grand Fenwick. We will call these income flows Grand Fenwick's *imported earnings*. Finally, some residents of other municipalities are employed in Grand Fenwick, and take their earnings with them back to their home cities, towns, and boroughs. We will call these income flows Grand Fenwick's *exported earnings*.

Let's say that the median earned income of a Grand Fenwickian who is employed full time is $20,000. Let us further assume that 1,000 Grand Fenwickians are employed within the borough, and 4,000 are employed elsewhere. Then, the domestic earnings of Grand Fenwick would be

$$\$20,000 \times 1,000 = \$20,000,000,$$

and the imported earnings would be

$$\$20,000 \times 4,000 = \$80,000,000.$$

Now let's assume that residents of only one other municipality, Sunnydale, work in Grand Fenwick. If the median earned income for an employed Sunnydale resident is $25,000 and 500 people from Sunnydale work in Grand Fenwick, we can calculate Grand Fenwick's exported earnings as

$$\$25,000 \times 500 = \$12,500,000.$$

---

[1] Earnings are estimated using U.S. Census data for median earnings in a commuter's residential municipality. This assumes that all residents in a municipality have a similar income distribution, whether they work in the municipality or commute long distances. This assumption is made more on the basis of data limitations than on any belief in its validity. However, the anticipated effect of this assumption is the understated interconnectedness of municipalities, since commuters may be more likely to have higher earnings than noncommuters.

Assembling the Blocks. The building blocks are used to generate key metrics for the income flows. After calculating domestic, imported, and exported earnings for each municipality within Allegheny County, we can begin to understand how income flows through the county. We continue the process by computing two additional measures for each municipality.

Captured earnings represent the total of all the paychecks brought home by *residents* of each municipality from jobs both inside and outside their home jurisdiction. So,

$$\text{Captured earnings} = \text{domestic earnings} + \text{imported earnings.}$$

Captured earnings are, in effect, the municipality's total earned income from all its residents who are employed full time, wherever their jobs may happen to be located. For Grand Fenwick, captured earnings would be:

$$\$20,000,000 + \$80,000,000 = \$100,000,000.$$

Generated earnings are the total of income from all *jobs* located within a municipality, whether held by residents or nonresidents of that municipality. So,

$$\text{Generated earnings} = \text{domestic earnings} + \text{exported earnings.}$$

Recalling that Grand Fenwick's domestic earnings were $20,000,000 and its exported earnings were $12,500,000, this would mean that Grand Fenwick's generated earnings total

$$\$20,000,000 + \$12,500,000 = \$32,500,000.$$

Ratios for Understanding Economic Interdependence. We can now use captured earnings and generated earnings to calculate two metrics of economic interdependence for each municipality in Allegheny County. First, we can measure what we call the *exported earnings ratio*, which is derived by dividing the municipality's exported earnings by its generated earnings. In essence, this measure reveals the degree to which a community is a source of income for the other municipalities in the county. A value of zero for a particular community would indicate that there are no commuters to a municipality, while a value of 1.0 would result if a nonresident held every job in the municipality. So, higher numbers indicate greater economic interconnectedness.

For a concrete example, the exported earnings for mythical Grand Fenwick would be

$$\text{Exported Earnings} \div \text{Generated Earnings} = \text{Exported Earnings Ratio}$$

$$\$12,500,000 \div \$32,500,000 = 0.385.$$

So Grand Fenwick exports 38.5 percent of all the income generated by jobs within its boundaries.

The second metric, the *imported earnings ratio*, measures how dependent each municipality is on income from "out-of-town" jobs. It is calculated by dividing the imported earnings of the municipality by its captured earnings; once again values closer to 1.0 indicate a greater degree of economic interdependency.

Again, as an example, Grand Fenwick's imported earnings ratio would be

$$\text{Imported Earnings} \div \text{Captured Earnings} = \text{Imported Earnings Ratio}$$

$$\$80{,}000{,}000 \div \$100{,}000{,}000 = 0.80.$$

This means that 80 percent of the total earned income flowing into the pockets of Fenwickians is generated by jobs located outside the borough's boundaries. This is a very high ratio of dependency, but as we will see, it would not be at all unusual for an Allegheny County community.

Residents and Commuters in Allegheny County

Before turning to the income analyses, it is helpful to examine the flow of workers across municipalities without any earnings attached to their movements.

Figure 1 shows the proportion of residents in each municipality in Allegheny County by workers who live and work in their municipality (who account for domestic earnings) and residents of the municipality who work somewhere else (the workers who account for imported earnings into a municipality).

On average, only 13 percent of residents work within their own municipality. Put another way; over 85 percent of workers on average in Allegheny County commute outside of their municipality to work. Of the 130 municipalities, only the City of Pittsburgh has more than 30 percent "domestic" workers, with 69 percent of its residents living and working within its boundaries.[2] Moon Township and Monroeville Borough have the next highest proportion of domestic workers, with 30 percent of their residents working in their municipalities.

Figure 2 shows the proportion of workers in Allegheny County municipalities for domestic (resident) workers in a municipality and those who commute into the municipality for jobs. As in Figure 1, this graphic illustrates a lot of exchange of commuters between municipalities in Allegheny County. On average, only 18 percent of workers live and work in a municipality relative to all workers.[3] Slightly more than half of the workers in Fawn and Reserve Townships are residents of those municipalities, although these represent relatively small numbers of workers (roughly 200 domestic workers for the combined townships). The

---

[2] It is important to note that, in general, the larger the geographical or population size area considered, the smaller the percentage of workers who engage in interregional movement to seek employment.

[3] Workers shown in Figure 2 include Allegheny County workers and workers from other areas outside the county who commute into municipalities.

Figure 1
Most Residents in Allegheny County Work Outside Their Municipalities

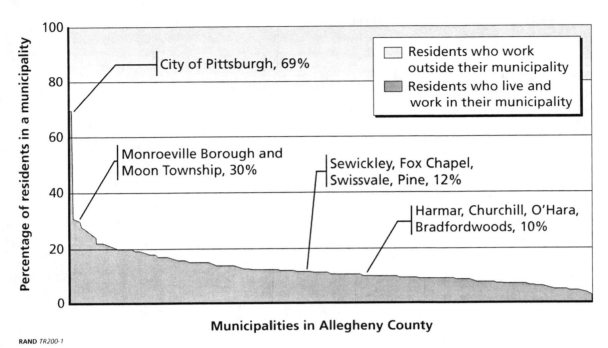

Figure 2
Most Workers in Allegheny County Municipalities Live Elsewhere

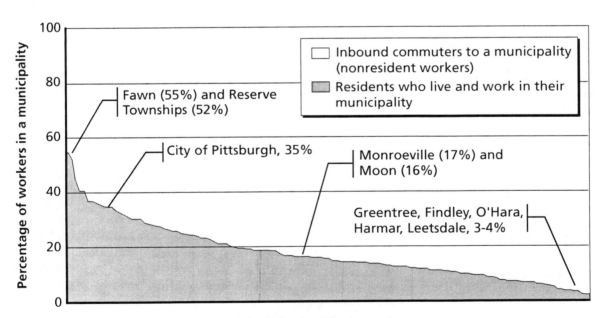

City of Pittsburgh has an estimated workforce of 35 percent residents and 65 percent non-resident commuters. More than 80 percent of the workforce in Moon Township and Monroeville Borough commute into these municipalities from other areas.

Attaching Income to Workers in Allegheny County Municipalities

With the insight that there is a lot of inter-municipal commuting, we begin the analysis by describing differences in the imported and exported earnings to examine patterns of income generation in Allegheny County. Some municipalities *export more income* to other areas than their residents import, meaning that more earnings leave the municipality than their residents bring in from other municipalities. These municipalities are referred to as net exporters of earnings. Other municipalities *export less income* than they capture, which means that residents bring in more earnings from jobs in other areas than the earnings of nonresident workers in that municipality take out of the municipality. These municipalities are referred to as net importers of earnings.

In Figure 3, municipal **net importers of earnings** are shown in solid shades from light gray to white for increasing earnings that are imported or brought into the municipality relative to earnings that are exported to other municipalities, yielding net surplus earnings for a municipality. Municipal **net exporters of earnings** are exporting more earnings to nonresident commuters than their residents import from other areas, yielding net deficit earnings for the municipality. These municipalities are shown in dotted shades of dark gray to black, indicating an increasing deficit between imported and exported earnings. Municipalities that are roughly even in their net earnings are shown in solid medium gray. These municipalities are roughly importing earnings equal to their exported earnings.

Figure 3 reveals interesting patterns of income in the county. Ten municipalities have estimated net exported (or deficit) earnings of more than $100 million, and 15 municipalities have estimated net imported (or surplus) earnings of more than $100 million.[4] These municipalities are presented in the table.

It is not surprising that the City of Pittsburgh is the largest exporter of aggregate earnings to other areas after subtracting out the imported earnings of its residents, yielding a net estimated earnings deficit of over $5 billion. The next largest sources of exported earnings in the county contribute estimated net exported earnings of about $350 million to commuters outside their municipalities. The first column of the table presents the ten municipalities with net earnings deficits of at least $100 million.[5] The right side of the table presents the top net importers of earnings in the county, again after subtracting the earnings of nonresident commuters. Fifteen municipalities have net imported earnings of over $100 million.[6] Note that total imported earnings do not equal total exported earnings since residents can earn income from municipalities outside of Allegheny County and nonresident

---

[4] As discussed in the appendix, no sample data are provided for small areas that do not meet specific criteria established by the Census Bureau. In Allegheny County, two municipalities fall into this category: MacDonald and Trafford Boroughs.

[5] Six municipalities have net deficits of over $50 million, and another eight have net exported earnings over $25 million.

[6] Five municipalities have net surpluses of over $85 million, and another 25 have net imported income over $25 million.

Figure 3
Some Municipalities in Allegheny County Have "Net Surpluses" of Earnings and Others Have "Net Deficits" of Earnings (Imported Earnings Less Exported Earnings)

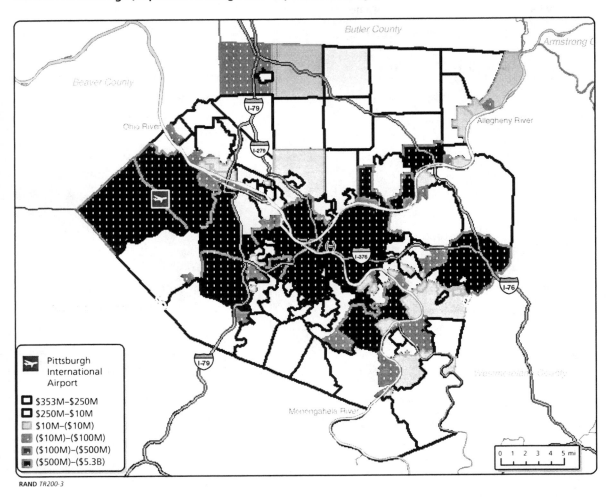

RAND *TR200-3*

Table
About One-Fifth of the Municipalities in Allegheny County Have Net Exported or Imported Earnings Over $100 Million (Total Imported Earnings Less Exported Earnings)

Municipalities with Net Deficits over $100 Million	Net Exported Earnings	Municipalities with Net Surpluses over $100 Million	Net Imported Earnings
Pittsburgh	*$5.3 billion*	Mount Lebanon, Penn Hills	$350 million
Monroeville, Findlay, Robinson, Green Tree	$300–350 million	Shaler, Upper St. Clair	$250–290 million
Moon, West Mifflin	$270 million	Franklin Park, Plum, McCandless, Baldwin	$220–240 million
O'Hara	$170 million	South Park, Bethel Park, Hampton	$170–199 million
Harmar, Collier	$110 million	Whitehall, West Deer, Fox Chapel, Elizabeth	$110–140 million

commuters can live outside the county, thus taking income outside the county. However, about 80 percent of Pittsburgh's net exports (more than $4 billion) go to commuters residing within the county.

Measuring the Interdependence of Earnings in Allegheny County

While the net surplus and deficit of aggregate earnings is important in understanding the importers and exporters of these earnings, the interconnectedness of municipalities for earnings can be better demonstrated using the exported and imported earnings ratios. As discussed earlier, the higher the imported earnings ratio, the higher is the proportion of income earned by residents in a municipality coming from jobs outside of the municipality. Similarly, the higher an exported earnings ratio for a municipality, the higher is the proportion of income generated by jobs in a municipality going to workers who are not residents of the municipality. Accordingly, as either of these ratios increases toward one, it indicates an increasing amount of interconnectedness or interdependence with other jurisdictions.

Figure 4 presents the distribution of exported and imported earnings ratios for municipalities in Allegheny County. The figure illustrates the degree to which municipalities in the county are economically dependent on others for earnings—both as importers and exporters for earnings for other municipalities.

Figure 4
Most Municipalities in Allegheny County Have High Imported and Exported Earnings Ratios

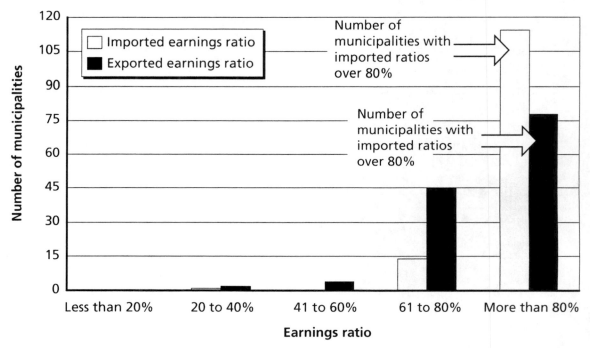

NOTES: The imported earnings ratio is the proportion of earnings coming into a municipality from outside jobs. The exported earnings ratio is the proportion of earnings in a municipality going to commuters.

The imported earnings ratios are striking in that all except one municipality have ratios higher than 60 percent. Indeed these are each 70 percent or higher, indicating that residents in these municipalities garner 70 percent or more of their earnings from outside their own municipality. The City of Pittsburgh is the anomaly, with an imported dependency ratio of about 30 percent, indicating that much of the earnings of Pittsburgh City residents are earned within its boundaries and not imported in from other areas.[7] Once again, the larger geographical and population size of the city may contribute to the smaller percentage of workers who engage in interregional movement to seek employment.

As shown in the bar graph, 114 municipalities have ratios of 80 percent or higher. This means that 80 percent or more of the earnings of residents in municipalities in the county are earned at jobs outside of that municipality. Figure 5 provides a view of the imported earnings ratios by municipality within the county. Here, dark gray and black indicate

Figure 5
Imported Earnings Ratios Show Municipalities Depend on Income from Others

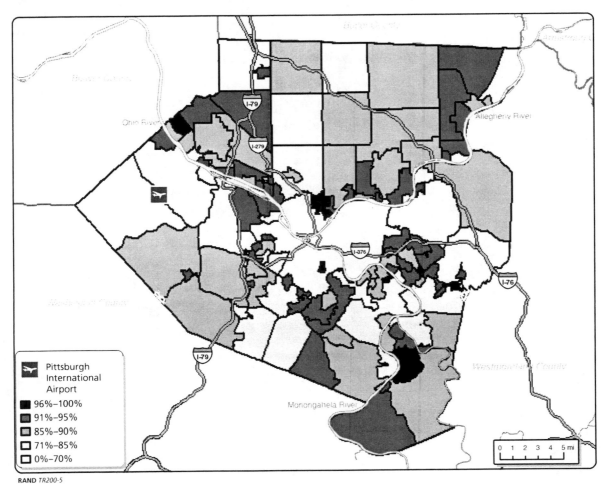

RAND TR200-5

---

[7] In absolute numbers, however, the city's imported earnings dwarf those of other municipalities. Estimated imported earnings of city residents are over $1.2 billion from other areas. The next largest "importer" is half this.

ratios of 90 percent or higher; lighter shades of gray indicate ratios between 70 and 90 percent; the white in the center shows the City of Pittsburgh with the only ratio less than 70 percent, with an imported earnings ratio of 30 percent.

As shown in Figure 4, the exported earnings ratios also tend to be high, with 124 municipalities having ratios over 60 percent, meaning that at least 60 percent of the income generated within these jurisdictions leaves their boundaries. Only two municipalities, South Versailles and McDonald Borough, have exported ratios under 40 percent (about 25 percent each). Figure 6 presents a graphical representation of the exported earnings ratios for municipalities in Allegheny County. Higher exported earnings ratios are represented in dark gray and black and lower ratios are shown in paler gray. The darker shading indicates that more of the earnings generated from jobs in a municipality go to nonresidents of that municipality, i.e., to nonresident commuters. Municipalities shown in white have exported dependency ratios less than 70 percent, with all but four municipalities having ratios greater

Figure 6
Exported Earnings Ratios for Municipalities Show High Levels of Income Leaving Boroughs

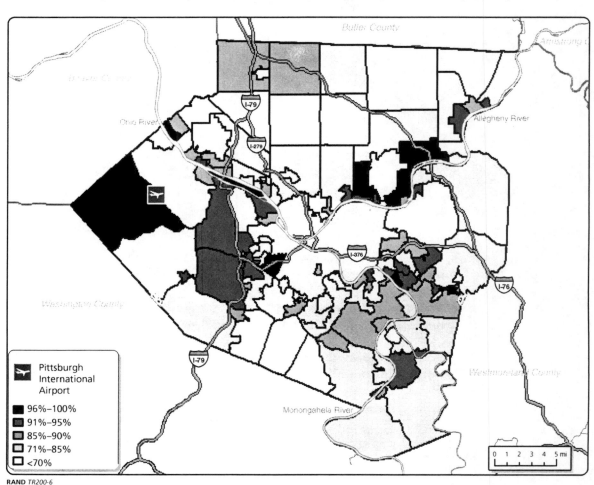

RAND *TR200-6*

than 50 percent,[8] meaning that well over half of the earnings generated in these municipalities are exported to other areas by nonresident commuters to that municipality.

Is the City of Pittsburgh Important for Municipal Income?

The analysis thus far has focused on how Allegheny County municipalities are economically interconnected based on earnings. We now turn to an examination of how jurisdictions are interconnected to the city. The City of Pittsburgh is the most financially distinctive municipality in the county, accounting for more than 35 percent of all exported earnings to the 130 municipalities combined[9]; nearly 80 percent of the city's exported earnings are distributed among the 129 municipalities in the county.[10]

We discuss the economic interdependency of surrounding municipalities and the city to examine the effect of earnings from the City of Pittsburgh on the *total captured earnings* of residents in a municipality—i.e., imported earnings plus domestic earnings—in terms of the *city earnings ratio*.

The *city earnings ratio* examines overall municipal dependency on Pittsburgh for economic earnings in the region through the ratio of earnings exported to the municipality from the city relative to the total earnings captured by the municipality. If a municipality has a significant source of commuter earnings from municipalities excluding the city and from its domestic earnings, then the importance of imported earnings from the city will be low. Accordingly, the city earnings ratio reveals how interdependent a municipality is on city earnings as a proportion of all earnings generated outside the municipality (i.e., earnings imported into the municipality from any other area) and domestic sources of earnings from residents who live and work there.

Figure 7 shows the distribution of the earnings ratio from jobs in the city for all municipalities. The bar chart reveals that all municipalities receive at least some portion of municipal earnings from the city relative to total income in a municipality. Four municipalities have city earnings ratios of 50 percent or higher, indicating that at least half of their income comes from the city. Sixty-three of the municipalities in Allegheny County have ratios higher than 30 percent. This means that nearly half of the municipalities in Allegheny County rely on earnings from jobs in the city for at least 30 percent of all earnings captured by that municipality. About one-third of the municipalities rely on city earnings for between 20 and 29 percent of both commuter and total municipal earnings. And about one-fifth of the municipalities rely on the city for less than 20 percent of all municipal earnings, with only nine of these municipalities having ratios under 15 percent.

Figure 8 provides a graphical illustration of a municipality's dependence on the city for earnings by captured earnings in the municipality. Higher ratios are depicted in darker

---

[8] Reserve and Fawn Townships each have ratios of about 45 percent; South Versailles Township and McDonald Borough have ratios of about 25 percent.

[9] The next largest generator of earnings represents fewer than four percent of all exported earnings among all such earnings in the county.

[10] The remaining 20 percent of the city's exported earnings go to residents outside of Allegheny County.

Figure 7
The City of Pittsburgh Provides Income to All Allegheny County Municipalities

Y-axis: Proportion of income from the city (in percentage)

Fox Chapel, Edgewood, Wilkensburg, Mount Oliver, over 50%

Churchill, Rankin, Baldwin, Braddock Hills, Mt. Lebanon, 42%

Franklin Park, Penn Hills, Sewickley Heights, West Homestead, Etna, Pleasant Hills, 36%

Hampton, Bethel Park, Kennedy, Harmar, 29%

Richland, South Fayette, Sewickley, Plum, 24%

Municipalities in Allegheny County

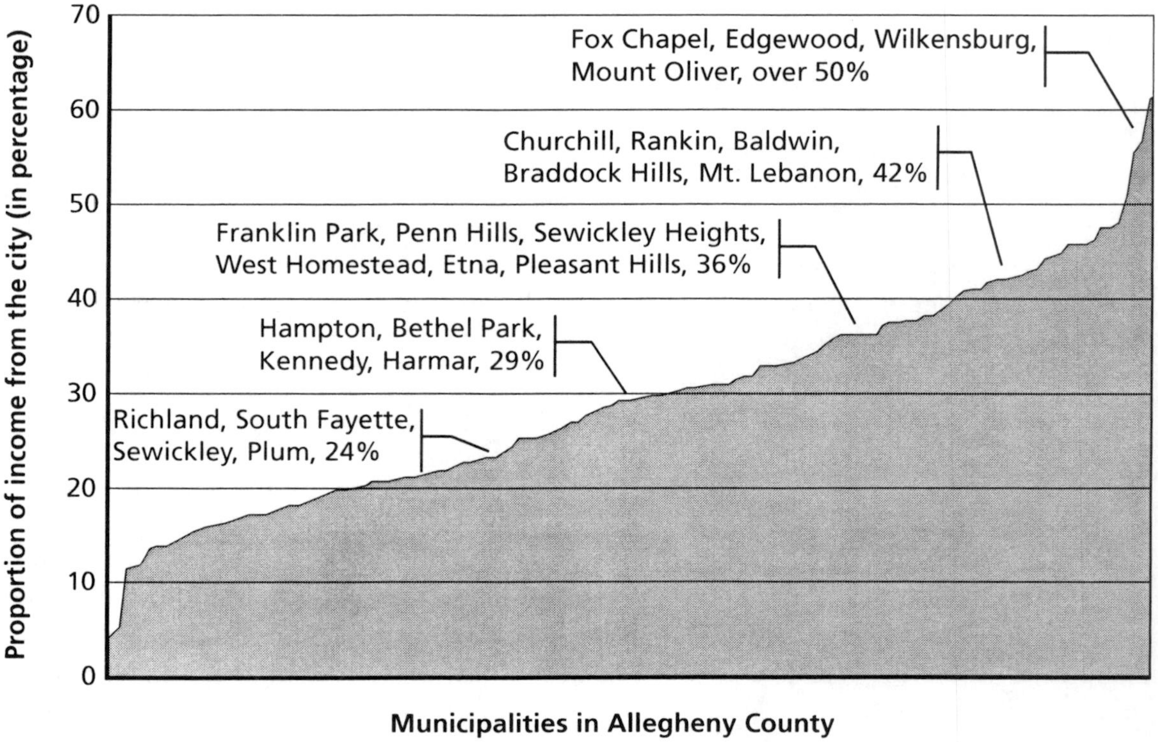

RAND *TR200-7*

shades of gray and black, becoming lighter with decreasing ratios.[11] Mount Oliver, Wilkinsburg, and Edgewood and Fox Chapel Boroughs each have ratios of 50 percent or higher. One striking feature of the graphic is the darker gray ring of municipalities surrounding the city and the similarly darker areas that follow key interstates and major routes north and south, showing the importance of city earnings for these communities. Equally interesting, however, are the locations of municipalities in lighter shades of gray, indicating a lower percentage of earnings stemming from the city. In particular, these include municipalities clustered south of the Monongahela River, far north of the Allegheny River, and on the western end of the county.

Conclusions and Observations

The descriptive analyses presented in this report show that Allegheny County municipalities are economically interdependent. Based on the commuting traffic into and out of each municipality, it is not surprising that each municipality exhibits high dependency ratios for both exported and imported earnings. It is remarkable, however, the degree to which municipalities are interconnected, with more than 80 percent of earnings on average leaving and entering jurisdictions across the county.

---

[11] The City of Pittsburgh is portrayed in white because, by definition, it cannot export earnings to its own residents.

Figure 8
Municipalities Vary in the Proportion of Earnings Received from the City of Pittsburgh

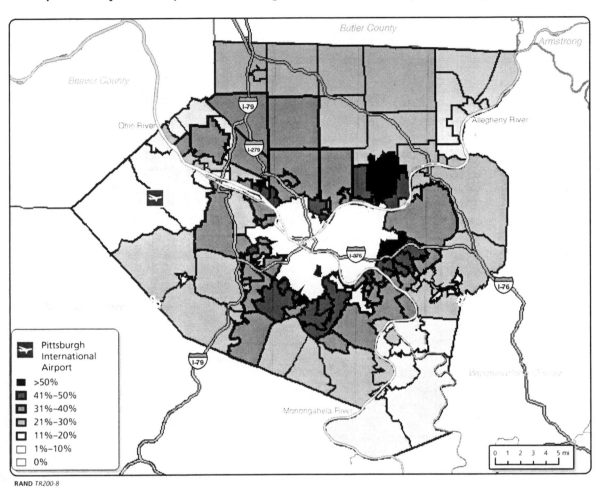

RAND TR200-8

The income dependencies indicate that the welfare of each municipality is unquestionably tied to the economic fates of their neighbors. As municipalities compete for jobs or residents within the county to bring these within their boundaries, then the dependencies may shift, although probably only minimally given the overall degree of interconnectedness. Indeed, even if the same people keep the same jobs and the net effect on individual income is zero, such intra-county competition would have an overall negative economic impact if there were costs to rearranging these slices, e.g., due to tax or monetary incentives to relocate. Because each municipality relies on its own tax base for revenues to provide services for its residents and businesses, they have an incentive to engage in this competition. The policy question is whether this is a good strategy for the economic health of the region—should these decisions be made locally by jurisdictions or is there a regional/county view that examines the existing pie?

We looked at income generated within the City of Pittsburgh to understand the impact of these earnings on municipalities in Allegheny County. The data show that the city is unquestionably the most significant generator of earnings for municipalities within the county. The next largest earnings generator in the county contributes only 10 percent of what the city supplies in earnings outside its own boundaries.[12]

Patterns of interdependence among the municipalities and the City of Pittsburgh suggest significant economic interconnections based on city-exported wages alone. The City of Pittsburgh sits at the center of the dense web of economic flows, providing jobs to 70 percent of its own residents and accounting for over 30 percent of total earnings for almost half of the municipalities within Allegheny County and at least 15 percent of the earnings for more than 90 percent of those in all municipalities in the county. These findings provide a basis to discuss the importance of the city to the economic viability of the region.

The fiscal turmoil in the City of Pittsburgh is creating many uncertainties. One result may be an exodus of residents and/or jobs to neighboring municipalities, rearranging the slices of the pie and further eroding the economic health of the city. It may also result in the loss of jobs to other regions if employers choose to locate or relocate in more financially sound locales. One policy issue is whether the city's status as the county's overwhelming exporter of jobs and income should earn the city special consideration in terms of recouping some of this revenue. In particular, what are the implications of the findings in this report for tax policy—is taxation a local or regional issue?

The discussions currently under way about city-county consolidation center on how to think and act more regionally to lessen inefficiencies and inequities caused by multiple layers of government. This same discussion can be extended to the 129 municipalities and the many other governance structures within the county. Regardless of how "fragmented" governance is within the county, Allegheny County is already deeply integrated economically, at least in terms of individual income, indicating that the county is a single "region" for employment. Which functions and services, then, truly are "local"? Residents choose their municipalities based on a number of factors, including access to work and the quality of housing, schools, and services. What model provides the ability to balance local preferences within a regional economic environment?

The question of what it means to make economic decisions as a region is particularly pressing today because of the fiscal pressures facing the city, county, and many of the municipalities. The descriptive analyses in this report begin to demonstrate the role that each municipality plays in contributing to the economic viability of its neighboring municipalities. The process of defining a region and a regional view is tied to these economic interconnections. This report provides a common understanding of how municipalities in Allegheny County are economically interdependent in order to allow meaningful conversations about what it means to be a region, and about which issues are local and which are more fundamentally regional.

---

[12] The City of Pittsburgh has total estimated exported earnings of about $6.6 billion. Monroeville Borough has total exported earnings of about $690 million, and Moon Township has about $610 million.

Data Sources for Analyses

Where do people live and where do they work? The answer to this question has important implications for economic interconnections within Allegheny County. It affects how wealth moves within the county and how the municipalities are interdependent.

This research uses publicly available data to provide estimates of where earnings are generated and where earners are domiciled within Allegheny County.

Commuter and Earnings Data

Both the commuter data and the earnings data contained in this report are derived from the U.S. Census 2000 Summary File 3 (SF 3), which is collected on a sample basis from the Census 2000 long-form questionnaire. SF-3 data, also known as "sample data," are obtained from questions asked of a sample, (generally one in six) of all households that have completed the Census 2000 short form. The responses from sample households reporting on long forms are weighted to reflect the entire population.

Commuter data were obtained from a customized data extraction of commuter data flows, which was prepared by the Pennsylvania State Data Center. This data extraction, which is based on the Census 2000 SF 3, provided information specific to the individual municipalities within Allegheny County and southwestern Pennsylvania region on each employee's place of residence and place of work.

Earnings data were culled directly from the U.S. Census web site, which provided sample median earnings on a municipality level. Earnings data are defined as "the sum of wage and salary income and net income from self-employment for full-time, year-round workers 16 years old and over who usually worked 35 hours or more per week for 50 to 52 weeks in 1999." The median divides the earnings distribution into two equal parts: one-half of the cases falling below the median and one-half above the median.

Because of these weighting procedures, each estimate based on the census long-form responses has an associated confidence interval. These confidence intervals are wider for geographic areas with smaller populations. The Census Bureau has determined that only geographical areas in which 200 or more long forms were completed provide sufficient "weighting areas" to produce good-quality estimates. Thus no sample data are provided for small areas that do not meet this criterion. Accordingly, this explains why data may not be available.

The Use of Median Earnings Data for Full-Time Year-Round Workers

The U.S. Census provides some alternative measures for earnings. In addition to median earnings, we considered using median total household income and per-capita income in our analyses. The Census data do not provide average earnings of full-time workers nor ranges (e.g., highest or lowest, percentile breakdowns, or confidence intervals) for any measure at a municipal level.

We did not elect to use median total household income since this includes payments from nonwork sources, for example, disability or social security payments and interest from investments. Median total household income, thus, could inflate the earnings of workers in poorer municipalities if a higher proportion of residents within a household receives some form of public assistance. Median total household income also could inflate the earnings of workers in more-affluent areas with significant household income from investment sources.

We also chose not to use per-capita income because it may be influenced by household size, and, like total household income, it may be influenced by unearned income sources. Accordingly, the data do not support an analysis of earnings flowing across municipal boundaries.

In the absence of actual earnings data for each worker, we opted to use median worker earnings for a municipality. This measure has advantages over the alternative measures since it is not affected by nonwork-related income and is not affected by high or low outlying earnings because the median divides the earnings distribution into two equal parts: One-half of the cases fall below the median and one-half above the median.

We believe that median worker earnings provide a conservative estimate of the extent of the economic independencies in Allegheny County. That is, we suspect that the use of median earnings underestimates earnings in nearly all of the municipalities. To illustrate, the median earnings reported for full-time year-round workers in the City of Pittsburgh is $28,777, meaning that one-half of workers earn less than this and one-half earn more. Since no worker can report earnings of less than zero dollars, the half of workers who earn less than the median are concentrated in a narrow range. In contrast, there is no upper limit in earnings above the median. Because of this, we suspect that average earnings in most municipalities would be higher than median earnings. Accordingly, we believe that the estimated earnings analyses presented in this report using median earnings reflect a lower bound of the actual income flows in the county.